A Soul Incarcerated

"From Pain to Passion to Freedom"

Memoir Vignettes with Art and Poetry

Mercedes Tidmore-Brown

Printed and Bound in the United States of America
Published and Distributed by:
Professional Publishing House
1424 W. Manchester Ave., Suite B
Los Angeles, CA 90047
www.professionalpublishinghouse.com
Drrosie@aol.com
323-750-3592

Cover Design: Richard Ike

Formatting: Alpha Enterprises

Illustrator: Martin R. Brown:

First Printing, March 2011
10 9 8 7 6 5 4 3 2 1
ISBN 978-0-9826704-6-0

Publisher's Note

Table of Contents

About the Author 7

About the Artist 8

Introduction.. 10

Chapter One...My Spiritual Journey 12

Chapter Two...Personal Statement....................... 15

Chapter Three...Reflection.................................. 18

Chapter Four...Relationships 26

Chapter Five ...An Inspired Relationship 30

POETRY AND PRAYERS 35

Can You See Me Walking Tall?............................ 36

Blame Me... 38

Who Is? 39

Be Very Careful 40

Get Away 41

Live!.. 42

Love Light.. 43

Love Yourself Instead.. 44

My Daughter 46

My Dreams 47

My Father Moses 48

Oh Lover Of My Soul Part II............................... 49

Powers and Principalities.. 50

Prayers 51

Prayer For Antwan.. 51

Ancestors Come Now 52

Recognition of Father/Mother God............................. 55

Shadows 57

Spirit 58

Sunshine.. 59

Surface Landmark Rearranged 60

Sweet Holy Spirit Mother Goddess 62

My Blessed Holy Mother God.................................... 63

Sweet Holy Spirit Mother God One 64

Sweet Holy Spirit Mother God................................... 65

Sweet Holy Spirit... 66

Thanksgiving 67

There Is A River Flowing.. 68

Know That You Are 69

What Color Is Love?... 71

I Do Shine 73

Journeying.. 74

O Lover Of My Soul... 76

The Whispers Of Maat.. 78

Thoughts and Reflections Of

Mother/Father God And Our Ancestors 80

Prayers To Mother God 82

My Beloved Sweet Holy Spirit Mother God 84

If You Were Me.. 85

Life Is Art.. 86

Prayer for My Sons 87

Dedication To My Mother

I would like to dedicate this work to my Mothers: The first Mother of the universe. The Mother of all Mothers, the Mother of all Life. The Nurturer and Sustainer of all life, whom I choose too call Mother-God. Secondly, I give honor and credit to my mother, Argusa Tidmore who has sacrificed and dedicated her life to being the nourishment for six children who have also suffered in many ways. But, mainly because she sacrificed her love and devotion to her son, whom has served over 35 years in the California Department of Corrections as an inmate, prisoner and property of the State of California. I have gained strength in her sufferings. Her only son was sacrificed to the prison yards and the prison guards who continuously work towards keeping him housed at the various prisons throughout the State of California.

ABOUT THE AUTHOR

Mercedes A. Brown is a life long learner and a native of Long Beach California. She attended the Long Beach Unified School District where she received her formal education. She received a Cosmetology License in 1974. After beautifying the hair and minds of many individuals, she decided to develop her own mind by studying at California State University Dominguez Hills where she received a B.A. in Philosophy in 1985; and a Certificate in Alcohol and Drug Counseling in 2003. In 2005, she received a Master of Science degree in Community Counseling Psychology from Springfield College of Los Angeles, she is currently attending CSUDH in the Marriage, Family and Therapy Department, where she is studying to become a licensed marriage and family therapist.

ABOUT THE ARTIST

Martin R. Brown is a native of San Diego, California. He received his formal education in both Catholic and public schools. Martin was interested in studying art; drawing, painting and metal sculptures at California State University San Diego and later at California State University Long Beach and California State University Dominguez Hills where he obtained a Masters. Martin's interest led him to make objects that related to designs of environments imagined and real in visual images and graphic arts, using materials as symbols of expression as he perceived.

After college Martin obtained employment as a teacher in Compton, California and later decided to go back to the CSULB to get his teaching credential in Special Education, with an emphasis in Developmental Psychology in the School of Education. He currently holds a Lifetime Teaching Credential; Fine Arts and Special Education subject K-12, and has been working with middle school children in literacy and math reasoning skills.

While working at Henry Clay Middle School in Los Angeles, CA, Martin befriended a colleague and neighbor by the name of Brenda Tidmore. Through their long time friendship, she decided to introduce Martin to her sister, Mercedes, after he lost his wife, to a long battle with cancer.

Martin and Mercedes shared something mystical, upon their first meeting. They shared a common interest in music, poetry, literature and art. A connection of their conceptual creative forces were ignited in their beings.

It was at that moment that the conceptualization of this work began to formulate and they compiled this vivid collection of poetry and visual arts. A marriage was formed and even now their marriage continues to conceive many new ideas.

8

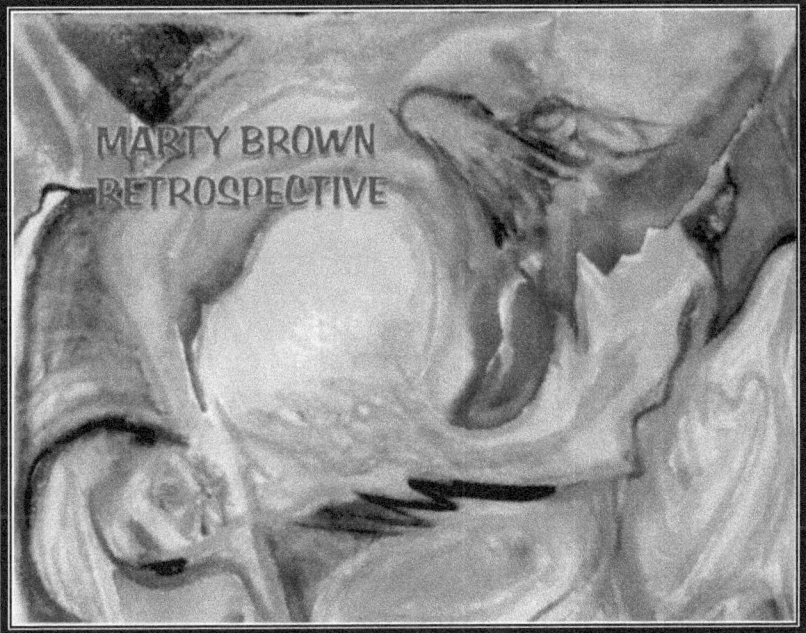

MARTY BROWN
RETROSPECTIVE

Introduction

I have watched my mother suffer in silence, pains of not having her son around to comfort her and reassure her that he is okay. I have witnessed my mother crying, tearless tears, and only being able to express herself with broken words of the pains and sufferings of really not knowing the future for her son. I have watched my mother grow old with the hope of being reunited with her son and the faith of seeing him at home around the dinner table, partaking in the blessings of being with family, friends and relatives. With that strength, hope, and faith, I am able to do the same as I await my son's return home from a fifteen-year sentence, just as I have in the past. Waiting and watching my eldest son return home from an eight-year sentence.

I must acknowledge and recognize my grandmothers from the past three generations. My grandmothers who had struggled with the pains of shame and guilt of the incarceration of their sons; living and dying in various prisons throughout the United States. I can only imagine how they suffered and died in silence while their sons were in confinement. Not being able to correspond or communicate with their loved ones after the news of their arrest must have been devastating. Not having the ability to read or write, not having access to telephones or the financial means to accept collect calls is un-thought of today. Oh how my soul sighs at the remembrance of them.

With the strength and remembrance of my ancestors and the recognition of the Supreme power of Mother-God, I humbly ask for guidance and direction in sharing my experiences within the context of this book. It is my hope that I am able to impart upon you the understanding of that part within all human beings that need to be loved and understood and the need to love and understand.

As a student in the Marital and Family Therapy Program at California State University Dominguez Hills, it is my hope that I will be able to learn to formulate an operative theory that will assist in the treatment and healing of individuals who are and have been affected by the psychological stress and trauma of incarceration. There are a few psychopathological diseases and disorders that are directly impacted by the mental functioning of the individuals and families who have been confined within cells of imprisonment. Although the family is not allowed to go beyond the visiting room of the prison facility, a mother or devoted family member's soul is affected by the thought of the loved ones' confinement. There are ways to address the issues that the individual and family unit, have to process the acceptance and understanding of incarceration and proceed with their daily aspects of living life. I will attempt to assist the concerned and affected family members impacted by incarceration in a variety of ways to help them accept and cope with the psychological struggles of incarceration.

Chapter 1

My Spiritual Journey

At a very early stage of my life I knew that there was something different about me. I used to entertain thoughts of life and death at a young age. I would lie on my bed, looking into space and think about God, angels, my parents, and would ask myself questions no one that I knew could answer. I lived in somewhat of an imaginary world, filled with spiritual accolades. As long as I can remember, I've always identified with my spiritual self. I can recall hearing an inaudible voice of God at a young age, possibly around seven years of age, speaking to my mind "the first shall be last and the last shall be first". While attending Christ Second Baptist Church weekly, I was also involved in visiting my uncles or brother in juvenile hall and jails with my family. As a child, I believed I had a heavy burden to carry, on a difficult path and journey. From religion to the law, music, philosophy and psychology in between; I have been influenced by these subjects and they have been intricate in my studies and being.

About 16 years ago, Maat presented herself to me in the form of a drawing. I began to research this figure and was drawn to the ASCAC conference at Southwest College. I believe it was then that I was introduced to Christ Unity Church under the guidance of Rev. Richard Byrd. This is a place that fulfilled my spiritual quest and answered many questions that revealed hidden treasures and secrets of the world that I live in.

Within the 16 years that I've been enlightened by the wisdom and the knowledge of my ancestors and my elders, I've been on a profound path. I won't go into details however; the journey began at birth and continues until this day. As I strive toward obtaining my second master's degree, I believe that I have a mission to fulfill in our community in the area of mental health therapy and well-being by providing emotional and psychological support and counseling to the members of our communities who have been impacted by posttraumatic stress and incarceration.

I believe I am (we are) to speak Maat, do Maat and present the principles of Maat, in every action of my (our) existence to be successful. I have recently filed the Articles to "N 2 Life Foundation" for the non-profit organization whose mission is to focus on decreasing the rate of recidivism for the ex-offender in the State of California and possibly throughout the Country. It is my plan and purpose to implement the principle of Maat: truth, righteousness, balance, order and harmony with Love in that program that will be designed to assist the ex-offender in staying out of prison.

Because I had been impacted by incarceration at a very tender age and am a mother whose uncles, brother and sons have spent over one hundred years in the State Prisons, I know that I have an obligation to my ancestors, family and community to make a positive contribution to society for my grandchildren, children, and children ad infinitum and to assist in healing and breaking the cycle of incarceration.

Another life goal that I have is to become a published poet and author. I have had a lot of life's challenges and issues that I have had to deal with and overcome. Along with these difficulties came life's lessons and victories. It is my hope and prayer to write about the therapeutic process of coping with various challenges and conditions that I've been afflicted with. I believe the spirit of Maat has been with me throughout the good and the not so good times in my existence and continues to speak to me and guide me. And so it is throughout the life and times of Mercedes Antoinette "Maat" Tidmore Wms.-Brown.

Chapter 2

Personal Statement

As a teenaged mother of African descent, I was never encouraged to complete high school or to attend college. I was looked down on and condemned for being that I am. I was discouraged for being anything other than a failure. Regardless of the negativity I received from my family and friends, there was an inner friend that resided within me and motivated me to want to learn, understand and know the secrets of life.

At the age of 18, I was the mother of one man's son and the wife of another man who was a heroine addict. My husband overdosed and died three months after we married. I was torn, traumatized and devastated. I did not know what to do. I felt there was no one I could turn to, nor talk with, that could help me to understand the hurt, pain and suffering I was undergoing. No one could identify with me as being a widow and a teenaged single mother.

As I reflect on my life and work experience, I have had to learn many hard lessons in my 55 years of living thus far. Many of the lessons I have learned have been very painful and traumatic. Some of the lessons have been valuable and a few have been pleasurable. Nonetheless, I have learned that there is a lesson to be learned in every circumstance and situation in life. I continue to realize this daily.

I have adopted a few sayings to continue to encourage myself as well as others. These sayings are "To live is to learn". "Life is learning"; and "Life is labor". These mottos keep me motivated and inspired to live more, learn more and do more.

The saying "to live is to learn" is one of the most valuable mottos that I continue to live by. As I think about the many schools and classrooms that I have attended; from the institutions of higher education to the grounds of 'Sidewalk University.' I have learned that there are many graduations I must attend in life. I have graduated from elementary school to high school, and from Beauty College to Long Beach City College. I have graduated from universities to many adversities in my life and from extended education to me now seeking more education and more lessons to learn.

The saying "life is learning" is another motto that I used to also keep me motivated to learn more. I enjoy learning and I do not believe that one can ever learn too much. Life is a learning experience in itself. Learning to live a meaningful life with purpose is one of my continuous goals. I have undergone many unpleasant and painful experiences on my jobs, which have inspired me to learn more about the field of psychology, counseling and mental health. The saying, "Life is learning" continues to inspire me to learn more about the proper policies and procedures and the correct ways to approach and handle various scenarios and situations in life.

In life, on and off the job, in the family and community there are many lessons to be learned and much work to be done.

My interpretation of this saying "Life is Labor" comes from my understanding that you have to work to live. There is a work I must do, a purpose I must achieve and a human need to serve. I believe my life's experiences have equipped me to study and work as a Marriage and Family Therapist to help others and to better serve my community. It is my goal to be of service and to serve with excellence.

The motto "life is labor" is a reminder that I must work to live a better life. By attending California State University Dominguez Hills and studying to become a licensed Marriage Family Therapist, it will enable me to become the best that I can be and it will also allow me to learn a few more lessons that will enhance my quality of life.

Chapter 3

Reflections

A s I look back and wonder how I got over, I must take a spiritual assessment of my growth and development as a Christian in Black America. Christianity is a major religion and practice by a nation of African American people who have had the need to reach out to a power greater than ourselves, to help us in our everyday life and the struggles we encounter on a daily basis. Circumstance and situations from A to Z, can summarize the need of the African "Negro" slaves to bow down and worship a God that we have been totally ignorant of. As a result of the many preachers that preach the doctrine of the Salvation of Jesus Christ, the Son of God whom died on the cross for our sins, Christianity is one of the main religions that have allowed the African American to be set free.

In my family and community, Christianity is more than a religion, it's been a way of life. It's been a social gathering for people in need of an outlet. It's been a place where families come together and share our lives and commonalities together. It was a way of life for many of my ancestors who had to work hard everyday to make it to the next day. It's been a way to restore strength, belief, trust, faith, and hope in God, Jesus Christ, and in self.

At the onset of my spiritual journey and search for my true self, I had gotten lost along the way. I started out on one path and ended up on another. When I stopped to find my way, I had to fall on my knees, go within and cry out in desperation for help. I will attempt to share with you an assessment of the spiritual journey I have been on in my quest for my spirituality. I will also attempt to share my experience as a Christian growing up in Long Beach, California.

As long as I can remember, I have been in the church. I sometimes wonder if I was conceived in the church because of my deep sense of spirituality and my spiritual awareness in all stages of my life. I was baptized at the age of five. Being baptized is being immersed in water as an indication of being cleansed and purified from sin. Being baptized also meant accepting Jesus Christ as my Savior. The frightening thing about being baptized was being immersed under water and becoming a new person. I was scared to death. But, somehow I made it through. I was able to join many auxiliary groups such as the Choir and the Usher Board after being baptized.

After being baptized it was said that you are open to being filled with the Holy Spirit or the Holy Ghost. Having the Holy Ghost was also known as being baptized with the fire. As I reflect on my spiritual journey/assessment, I would have to say that I was filled with the Holy Ghost fire after I became an adult. As a child, I can remember pretending that I had the Holy Ghost and would start shouting. Shouting consisted of yelling in a loud voice "Thank you Jesus or Hallelujah" as though you were screaming and crying. One would jump and dance as though his/her soul was on fire. Another form or aspect of being filled with the Holy Ghost consisted of speaking in tongues. Speaking in tongue was like speaking in an unknown language. It was said that when one is speaking in tongue the Holy Spirit is communicating and comforting the soul. Crying was also a way of being filled with the Spirit. It was said that crying was a way the Spirit cleansed the soul.

19

As a child I loved to sing just as my mother did. My mother encouraged me to sing and would help me to sing the songs learned at choir rehearsal. The choir director, Mrs. Gaskin, thought I had a good enough voice to sing lead. One of the songs I led was "It's me, It's me, It's me oh Lord, standing in the need of prayer". I can truly say that ever since those words rolled from my lips, I have been standing in the need of pray as I remain in the need of prayer until this day.

In my family, religion played a major role in our everyday lives. It shaped our thinking by giving us meaning to our daily existence. We lived by the Ten Commandments. The Ten Commandments is the foundation of our religious values and beliefs and behaviors that shaped my every thought and existence. Thou shall have no other gods before me. Thou shall not make thee any graven image. Thou shall not bow down thyself unto them or serve them. Thou shall not take the name of the Lord thy God in vain. Thou shall keep the Sabbath day to sanctify it, six days thou shall labor and do all thy work, on the seventh day is the Sabbath of the Lord thy God: in it thou shall not do any work. Honor thy father and thy mother, that thy days may be prolonged. Thou shall not kill neither shall thou commit adultery neither shall thou bear false witness against thy neighbor. Neither shall thou desire thy neighbor's wife, neither thou covet thy neighbors' house, his field or his manservant or his maidservant, his ox, or his ass or anything that is thy neighbors.

Being a Christian has its benefits in establishing values, morals and positive behaviors in the home, community and Society as a whole. On the opposite side, the Ten Commandments has its dualities. Just as it is written, thou shall not commit adultery, and there is the adulterous. Just as it is written, thou shall not kill and there is the murderer. Another revelation that occurred to me is how one of the commandments says thou shall not covet his neighbor or anything that he has. This is the foundation of a lot of crime; wanting what belongs to others. This is the main reason why some of my dearest family members are currently serving time in prison or awaiting trial. The breaking of the laws of the Ten Commandments leads to the dysfunction of the family and the consequences of crime and punishment.

Given these instructions as our rules for engagement, some of these very commandments are the reasons for the destruction of my family of origin. My father Moses Tidmore, was a very hard working man that provided his family with a modest lifestyle by working 12-16 hours per day. He provided his family with all the material necessities and more. However, he was unavailable emotionally and spiritually for the family. I had a problem with my father for a number of reasons. My father insisted that my sisters and I go to church weekly with our mother even though he rarely attended church with us as we were growing up. At the most formative years of our lives, he only attended church a few times that I can remember. I became angry with him for not participating in the religious services and activities. He did not practice what he preached.

While growing up, my father only attended church with the family, his wife and children less than four times that I can remember. On the other hand, my mother was extremely involved in the church. She had a beautiful singing voice and she was even more beautiful in spirit. My mother was a member of two choirs at Christ Second Baptist Church in Long Beach, the Gospel Choir and the Inspirational Choir. She attended church two times on Sunday, morning and evening services. Almost everyday of the week our mother and her five children were going to church for one reason or the other; prayer service, little kids prayer service, Bible study and choir rehearsal kept us busy. On Wednesday nights, my mother would attend mid-week Prayer Service while I was at home

21

playing church with our neighbors. On Saturday, I attended Junior Usher Board where I learned and practiced being an Usher for ten years. This was a regular routine for me. It was though we lived in the church.

My father was verbally abusive to my mother and his children. I can remember my father and mother arguing about momma spending too much time at church and how she would give the preacher her money. My father would never support my mother financially in her religious endeavors, nor did he support his children in their social functions and activities at the church. But, he made sure I attended church every Sunday. According to my mother, my father committed adultery on more than one occasion. This was a fundamental breaking of the law of the Ten Commandments.

Christianity was the religious choice of my family. Momma's only son, my brother, AKA Ali, is the eldest of the six children. He did not believe in the blonde hair, blue-eyed image of Jesus Christ whom pictured was hung on every wall, in every family members and friend's household. I understood little about Jesus except that he died on the cross for my sins and he died for my salvation. In my understanding of Jesus I was told he was the father, the son and the Holy Ghost. However, my brother rebelled against this knowledge.

My brother Fred (Ali) was diagnosed as a borderline genius. He would never go to church like momma would expect. Momma spoke of him acting terrible in church as a toddler stating he was always saying he wanted to go outside. When we became adolescents, he would always act like he was going to church. Momma would look around to see if he was in church and once they made eye-to-eye, contact he would get up and walk out of the door. He got to the point where he would walk into one door and out of the other.

After awhile momma was wise to what he was doing. She would ask me, "Did you see your brother in church today?" I would hesitate and knowingly lie for him. I was caught in the middle of the two of them. Fred would ask me to tell him what the preacher's sermon was about. I answered I didn't know and he would keep asking me until I had to tell him something. "Jesus loves us and he died for our sins," I would tell him. I believe that was the beginning of my ministry. Fred later became a Muslim and adopted the holy name of Ali.

Reverend Herman Gore was the pastor of the church. He was very good looking and attracted many people to the church. He also had many dedicated followers. He was a man of Indian descent. He appeared to be very spiritual and performed many ceremonies and rituals. Rev. Gore often told of his encounters with the Spirit of God and his visions he had from God. Once he spoke of being knocked out in the spirit at home for days. He had a mystical affect on me and probably every woman in the church. Rev. Gore appeared to have a positive and negative affect on the members of the church and on our family and community.

While growing up in the church, I memorized the books of the Bible yet my understanding of God had not increased or developed. I continued to attend church weekly without any better knowledge or understanding of God than I did when I first started attending church as a child. I had a lot of unanswered questions about my religion.

At the age of 16, I became pregnant and my family was disappointed and ashamed of me for being an unwed mother. I felt like I was ousted from the church. Instead of studying the Bible and concentrating on school, my mind was preoccupied with motherhood. Little did I know I was headed for a life of heartache and pain. My spirituality took a 360-degree change. I attempted to explore and learn of many aspects and denominations of religion. I was on a path, a spiritual journey in which I would elevate my conscious mind and spiritual soul.

- Age 0-15 attended church 4-5 days a week
- Age 16 – became pregnant attended church less
- Age 17 – Introduced to Islam
- Age 23 – Started College Introduce to Philosophy and World Religions
- Studied Seventh Day Adventist, Jehovah Witness, Science of Mind, Church of Religious Science, African Religion, Egyptian Studies, Catholicism, Johrei and more.

As a child I had a spiritual awareness that came from deep within. My spirit would have me ask questions about God and Jesus to my mother that she could not answer. She would always tell me not to put a question mark where God has put a period. As a custom it was not appropriate to ask questions about God in our household.

Today, in my quest to understand my spiritual heritage, I continue to ask the questions and continue to search for a greater awareness and relationship in my understanding of God. Religion continues to play an integral part in my family of origin. I'm grateful for the Christian values and behaviors I learned as a child. For this knowledge will never be imparted from my mind or my heart.

I believe our family has been plagued by a lack of knowledge and understanding of the God we serve and the impact of the dysfunctions and the misunderstandings it has had on the family has manifested in behaviors such as adultery, disobeying our parents, lying, addiction, murder and other crimes and punishments. As a direct result of the lack of

24

knowledge and understanding many of us remain in these current situations.

O Gracious Mother God, I thank you and glorify you for your love and tenderness. I thank you for your presence in my life and my soul. I shine in your blessedness. Thank you for your radiant light that heals us and protects us always. I magnify you in your holiness. AMEN

Chapter 4

RELATIONSHIPS

In my fifty-five years of living, I have experienced and encountered all types of relationships. Some of the most significant relationships that I have been in were abusive and violent relationships, sexual and platonic relationships, distant and close relationships and parent/child relationships. These are just some of the type of unhealthy relationships that I have had with individuals. I have had a few positive, encouraging and enlightening relationships on other levels, but between the age of fifteen and fifty-one, for thirty-six years, I had been exposed to and learned some of the worse lessons of my life regarding domestic violence and abusive relationships.

Most of the intimate and personal relationships I have been in were dysfunctional, full of emotional trauma and turmoil, physical and verbal violence and abuse, and not a lot of happiness. Very few of the relationships were satisfying on a spiritual and mental level. Even less, were pleasing physically or sexually. These relationships lacked the self-love and esteem, honor and trust that one needs to sustain a loving and healthy relationship. I will attempt to share with you the understanding I have of "Relationships" and the three most important relationships that exist for me today.

The root of the word relationship is to "relate". To be in a relationship is to relate to another, or to have relations, or to be connected by blood or marriage. It also means to narrate, recount; establish relation between; have reference or relation to. In order to relate to another there must be some form of communication and dialogue between another. After it has been establish that there is connection between one and another, a relationship is formed.

When I was young, I lacked the knowledge and wisdom to know what true love was all about. The most destructive relationship I've been in was an addictive type of love. I wanted to believe that I was truly in love. I did not know what love truly was. I was in love with love. I lacked the knowledge and understanding of myself, which made it impossible for me to fully and wholeheartedly have a relationship with another based on hope, wisdom, creativity, courage, spirituality and responsibility. These relationships lacked the balance that was needed to be fully functional and healthy.

One of the most fulfilling and satisfying relationships I have had is with my maker and creator, whom I choose to call Mother/Father God. This relationship is one of the most sacred and important relationships in all of the world and humanity that I can fully and intimately embrace. Because of the relationship I have developed with my higher power, I have been able to do all things through this power, which has strengthened me. I've been protected from all hurt, harm and danger, even though in my domestic violent relationships, I have had my teeth kicked out, blackened eyes, damaged bones and nerve endings, kicked down, knocked down, and was put down all around. I've been close to death in my life and at those times I could feel the eyes and hands of God watching over me and protecting me at that very hour. I've come to realize that because of my relationship with this divine power, I have been saved and kept alive for this very day.

This relationship began within the first five years of my life. As I reflect on the closeness of this spiritual connection that I was drawn too, I contribute it to my mother who made sure her children where baptized and participated in the church activities at least three days during the week and all day on Sundays. However, she was not responsible for the intimate relationship that I developed with my personal savior. This relationship came about as a direct result of my attunement to a spiritual power at a young age. Before the age of eighteen I had encountered some life threatening incidents and I had no one to turn to or to help me but a power greater than myself.

Another important relationship I had to develop and grow to love was one with 'self.' The backbone of a successful relationship is the existence of love. To know and love thyself is necessary to have self-esteem and confidence. In the process of developing a relationship with my-'self' and learning to fully and wholeheartedly accept and appreciate myself was not very easy. It took a long journey for me to embark upon. Retraining myself to relate differently to myself than my perpetrator and abusers did, was tedious. I was programmed to think the worse about my total self. I was taught to think as the perpetrator secretly thought.

I learned to use 'self-talk'. I learned to turn my thoughts around and adopt the attitude that I was fearfully and wonderfully made. Developing a relationship with myself has allowed me the privilege of embracing myself and loving myself unconditionally. By learning to love me for me, I have given myself permission to be truly loved by another. Because I now love and honor myself, in return I am truly loved and honored.

At the age of fifty-one, I met a man who would soon come to be known as my third husband. I really did not know how to relate to him or to be in a healthy relationship. However, I decided it was time to learn. Our line of communication was open and vast. We had deep conversations. It was then that I learned we had much in common.

We both had master degrees, his in Art and Education, mine in Human Service and Psychology. We conversed about religion, philosophy, music and the arts. He read poetry to me, I wrote poetry to him. We had both been divorced and had both lost our spouses to death. We took walks on the beach to watch the sunset and weekend trips to get away from the city. What I was most attracted to was the way I felt when I was with him. He made me feel like a queen. He was very attentive to my needs and gave me the utmost honor and respect.

After all the unhealthy relationships that I had come to know, I decided to do something much different than I ever did before. I got involved with a gentleman outside of my race. I am learning to relate to him on a different level. We relate to the mind, body and soul of our beings. I feel secure and happy when we're together. He speaks lovingly without words of abuse. We are inspired by each other to fulfill our goals and to become the best that we can be. We are connected and in-tune with each other as we relate to each other. Our relationship is built on honesty, harmony, trust, honor and healing. The relationship I am in with my husband continues to grow into something unique, and different. He understands the trauma that I've gone through in the past 36 years and has encouraged me to heal. As a result, our love continues to blossom and grow into something beautiful, inspiring and creative.

Chapter 5

AN INSPIRED RELATIONSHIP

My relationship with my brother has been very inspirational and motivating. My life has been impacted and shaped by various aspects of his incarceration. The experiences that I gained in going to court with him, staying connected by writing to him and accepting collect phone calls, sending him money orders, stamps and quarterly packages, and traveling to remote places in California better prepared and equipped me for the challenges that I would have to go through 20 to 30 years later with my own sons.

I've traveled thousands of miles, to various prisons through out the State of California. I have visited my loved ones at Chino, Folsom, San Quentin, Lancaster, Centinnela, Calipatricia, Corcoran, Avenal, Tehachapi, Donavon and Pelican Bay State Prison. From the bottom of California to the tip, top of California, I've been on a journey. For the past forty-eight years my relationship with my brother has influenced my life in many positive aspects and it has also created deep emotional pain, anger and depression.

When I was eight years old I can remember visiting my brother at the Los Angeles County Juvenile Hall and Detention Centers. On the week ends or whenever time allowed, my mother would gather her daughters together, pack a lunch and off we would go to spend the day with her only son, and our only brother.

30

I don't ever remember seeing momma crying for her son, but I would cry for hours for her. I felt the pains of leaving a child behind, not knowing what one-day to another, would bring. I would pray for his health, and safety, asking God to protect him. It was not easy or fun being the oldest daughter. I had to take on a lot of responsibility in the home and be there for my mother. The emotional pain she suppressed, I expressed. I had to be there to support her emotionally and psychologically. I had to help her with my sisters.

As the years went by it became a continuous cycle. My brother continued to go in and out of jails and eventually he went to prison. In 1975, he was convicted for attempted murder and robbery and sentenced to twenty years to life in the California State Department of Corrections. I was devastated and in shock by the event. I cried for my brother, I cried for my mother and I cried for myself. When he walked out of the courtroom it was like a death. I grieved for years.

The difference between losing a loved one to death and being sentenced to twenty years to life in prison is that you are able to visit with your loved one and see them alive, moving, walking, talking, laughing and breathing. When on the other hand, a loved one dies or when there is a death in the family you are able to mourn and grieve for a period of time and move on with your life. You can visit with your loved one at the cemetery on their birthday and holidays or you can choose not to visit the gravesite at all. That is the difference between being dead and buried alive. Having a family member incarcerated is like being buried alive. The pain and sorrow can become unbearable, sometimes to the point of sickness unto death.

Being supportive of my loved one while being incarcerated has consisted of many different actions and good deeds, on many different levels. It's expensive being there for them. The

31

time and money that it takes to visit for the weekend can cost more than a weeks salary for me. The price of gas, food and accommodations are the initial cost of the travel expenses. When entering the visiting room, you are allowed to bring up to fifty dollars per adult and ten dollars per child for the vending machines.

There have been times when I've been unemployed for long periods. During those times it was very difficult to even write letters to let him and my oldest son know how bad I was doing, how tuff it has been and how sorry I was. Who wants to hear news like that? I'm more than positive that is why so many prisoners do not have the support of their low-income, poverty stricken families.

As a direct result of my relationship with my brother, I have been divinely inspired and intellectually motivated. My relationship with him has influenced the way that I view the world. My relationship with my brother has encouraged me to develop my relationship with God and to further my educational growth. I had decided that as long as he was incarcerated, I would go to an institution of higher education.

Being a student at the (CSU) California State University is somewhat comparable in my mind to my brother being a prisoner or an inmate at the CSP, the California State Prison. Due to the incarceration of my brother, I believe I've been sentenced to the institution of higher education. I continue to thrive towards achieving my highest level of education. After his eleventh year of imprisonment, I vowed to myself that I would remain in college until his freedom. After many challenges and many changes, I became weary and grew tired.

After attending different colleges for ten years full time, I dropped out of school. I thought about the commitment I had made to myself to remain in school as long as my brother remained in prison. I could not take it any longer my soul grew older and tired. It became sick with emotional and psychological infirmities. My eldest son was now in the same position as my brother. After the mental turmoil of his incarceration, I began to self medicate. I had developed Cirrhosis of the soul, a soul incarcerated.

The psychopathology of a soul incarcerated, consist of a co-morbidity of mental and emotional disorders, a psychological disease of the family. The effects of incarceration on the family has long term consequences. The family is co-incarcerated with the prisoner. Isolation, inability to sleep and eat, irritability, lack of concentration, tearfulness, can be the symptoms one is faced to cope with when one's family member is initially incarcerated.

Through out my life's experiences, my relationship with my brother has kept me spiritually connected to father God and grounded to mother earth. However, there was a period in my life when I had lost everything that I owned, but my faith in God. I had even found myself disconnected from my brother. I had become angry with him for spending the most important part of his adult life locked away from his family. I had even become angry at the California Department of Corrections and the Parole Board for not giving him the corrections or rehabilitation that he should have received to be paroled back into society. My anger and depression had gotten the best of me. I had to help myself and heal myself. I had to develop my self-awareness, knowledge and esteem.

By the age of eighteen years, I had experienced some very traumatic events in my short life. I was undiagnosed with post-traumatic stress disorder, anxiety and depression. During my struggles, and all of my ups and downs, my brother was there in spirit and in prayers.

His letters of hope and encouragement inspired me to dig out of the depths of my depression and reach for higher heights. His prayers have moved me to places I would have never gone or seen had it not been for the inspired relationship we have as siblings. Because of his incarceration, I have been able to go places with him in heart and mind so that I could share with him an aspect of life that he could only imagine and see behind bars, through my eyes.

After thirty-seven years in prison, I was sure that he should have been released by now. In the past after each denial from the parole board I would go into a deep state of sadness, a relapse in my thoughts and reactions. The symptoms would soon begin sleeplessness, loss of appetite, crying often, inability to concentrate, irritability, and more. I had to learn how to cope with the denial and to better accept the reality of his continuous confinement and thoughts that I will never give up on the hopes and beliefs of his release from prison.

My relationship with my brother has prepared me for the cycle of incarceration that my sons would have to endure as well. In their incarceration my soul has been sentenced in the psyche. In the psychological aspect of my soul being incarcerated, I have learned to free my mind and my soul. I have had many spiritual awakening while developing my mind. I have sought ways to embrace my journey and look for the good in every situation in my life. Because of my brother's endurance and his ability to exercise his faith as a Muslim, praying five times a day, fasting and studying diligently, he has inspired me to continue on my path of my spiritual enlightenment and on the educational journey which allows my soul to be free as a dove.

As my spirit soars from pain to passion to freedom, I am determined to attain to the heights of my educational goals and life's purpose. I will remember not only the struggles of my brother and my sons, but of all the inmates and prisoners who will never have the opportunity to travel beyond the visiting rooms in the State Prisons of America.

Poetry And Prayers

Sentiments From And For Incarcerated Souls

Can You See Me Walking Tall

Can you see me walking tall
With my head up high
Shoulders held back
Straight and erect
I'm preparing myself to fly.

Can you see my soul is soaring
Reaching every goal
Turning every stumbling block
Into stepping stones.

Can you see me climbing higher
Reaching for the top Knowing
Together we can make it
If we just don't stop.

Can you see us going the, distance
Further than we could have dreamed
Traveling not against the currents
On a tide moving…floating…
Towards our place upstream.

Do you know which ever route
That we may choose to go
Traveling onward land or sea
Even as a bird in the air
There is one thing we must do
Leave behind the baggage of doubt.

Blame Me

You can blame me if you want to. It's quite all right with me. It only verifies the confirmation of the power that God has given to me.

You can blame me if you want to, put all the responsibility on me, for I am a strong black woman and I am free to be.

The power within my mind is the same as the creative energy in the universe bringing about a transformation not only for myself yes, but for you as well.

Blame me for the beauty in the entire world that you see, blame me for the making of all the Birds and the Bees. One thing you must realize is the essence of my ability.

I speak that which I dream of, call it forth, and it will be the power of the words that I speak have created you and me. So blame me for the problems that you say I create and I will be responsible for the goodness that formulates.

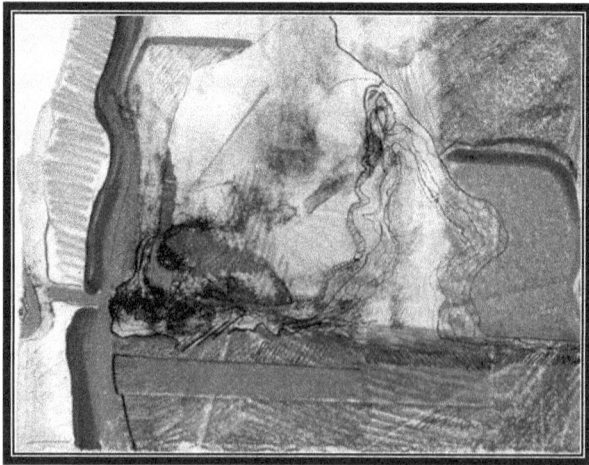

Who Is?

He who is?

She who is?

How can it be one without the other if it wasn't for thy mother?

The one is the mother, and the other is the father.

And so it is in thy praise and worship

The interaction with thy mother, and thy father,

As the one with the other

And so it is!

Be Very Careful

Be very careful of the vows that you make and all that you say. Is it any wonder why things are that way? Never again will I vow to another that I will love honor and obey whatever one may do, think, or say! In the eyes of my lover, whose heart is for another?

Never have a kind word that he would utter is it any wonder why things are that way? If he can only criticize and tell you fictitious lies, should you love, honor and obey whatever he may say? If he can only lower your self worth, put you down beneath the earth. Can you rise above the ground without feeling put down? Be very careful!

GET AWAY

Keep a low profile got to
Stay away for a while
Get off the scene cause
I don't need to be seen

Changing my direction
Making new connections
Seeking my God's instruction
Open to her corrections

I have heard the call
Must heed and not
Stall, whether I lay low
Or stand tall it's time to
Get away from it all

LIVE!

*Live and Let Live
Each day as it comes
Accept everything that
God has done*

*Do not fret yourself
Because of what you think
Should have been done
Be grateful for all things
Whatever may become*

*Be not critical
Of the choices one makes
Rejoice and be thankful
For it is s/he who creates*

*So Live and Let Live
For goodness sake
And accept the things
That can't be changed!*

*For all things truly
Work together for
The Good!*

"LOVE LIGHT"

Lord, let your love light shine
In the eyes of our darkness
May your love light, light up
Our eyes to see your light shine
In each and every one of us

Lord, let your love light shine
With Love throughout our lives
May we see your spirit
Each and every night

Lord, let your love light
Radiate in everlasting truth
It's because of your truth
And Divine light that we
Can be Free

May your spirit of truth
And light, light up our spirits
Of truth and light
Because in our darkest hour
Always comes your love light

With Love and Light

"LOVE YOURSELF INSTEAD"

SEEK NOT TO BE LOVED BY ANOTHER
LOVE YOURSELF INSTEAD.
ENJOY THE COMPANY OF YOUR INNER-SELF.
HOLD YOURSELF AND LOVE YOURSELF INSTEAD
LOOK IN THE MIRROR OF YOUR EYES,
SEE AND KNOW THE BEAUTY THAT RESIDES.

KISS YOURSELF, HUG YOURSELF, TRULY BE GOOD
TO YOURSELF INSTEAD.
BECOME YOUR FOREMOST LOVER BEFORE
YOU SHARE YOUR LOVE WITH ANOTHER
WALK BY YOURSELF, TALK TO YOURSELF
GET TO KNOW AND LOVE YOURSELF INSTEAD

TO LOVE SOMEBODY ELSE,
MORE THAN YOU LOVE YOURSELF
IS VERY DETRIMENTAL TO THE SPIRITUAL
ASPECT OF YOURSELF
TO LOVE ANOTHER BEFORE YOURSELF INSTEAD
NOT LONG WILL LOVE LIVE BEFORE IT'S DEAD!
SO! HOW CAN YOU TRULY LOVE ANOTHER?

WITHOUT LOVING YOURSELF INSTEAD!

LOVE,

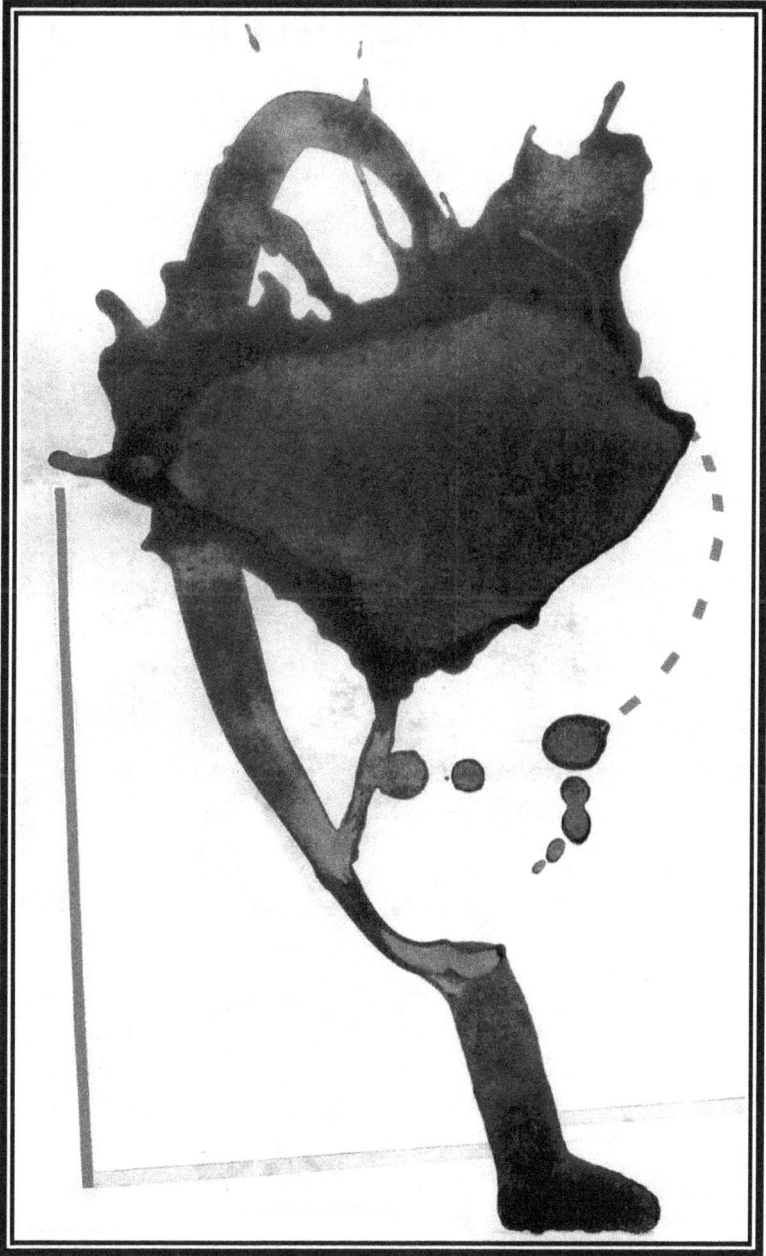

MY DAUGHTER

HOW I WISH I COULD TELL YOU
HOW GOOD AND SWEET LIFE IS
I THINK OF ALL THE PAINS I HAVE
HAD TO SUFFER AND IT HAS NOT
BEEN EASY

THERE IS ALWAYS WORK TO DO
OUR WORK IS NEVER DONE
NO MATTER WHAT TIME IT IS
IT NEVER STOPS LIKE THE
TICKING OF LIFE'S CLOCK

WHEN I THINK OF ALL THE
NECESSITIES THAT A GIRL AND
WOMAN NEEDS, IT IS NOT CHEAP
BEING A WOMAN AND NEVER IS
IT FREE

THERE ARE ALWAYS THINGS ON
OUR MINDS WE ARE THE MOTHERS
OF MANKIND NEVER CAN WE REST
BECAUSE, MY DEAR, THE POWER OF,
THE WOMAN IS ALWAYS BEING PUT
TO THE TEST

IF I CAN SHARE ANY SOLACE AT ALL
IT IS A COMFORTING FACT TO KNOW
GOD CREATED US THE GREATEST OF
ALL.

DEDICATED TO MY DAUGHTER
"DAAIYAH"
1994

My Dreams

My Desire is something
More than I Dream
I can perceive only a glimpse
Of my dreams and desires
That long to manifest
Itself on the outside
Of me in its physicality
If only I can dream

My Dreams will evolve
And they turn themselves
Into something more than
I can understand in the
Conscious state of my beings
Bringing forth the latent desires
Of my soul buried in the
Spirituality of my dreams

When I live my dreams
And dream of my life
I will create what has not
Been created, sing the
Song I have yet to sing
And write the unwritten
Words of the Sweet Holy Spirit
Mother God in my dreams

P.S. Your dreams will evolve
Into something beautiful
Only when you open your
Mind's eye and dream

My Father Moses

A hard working wise man
Not easy to understand
Because of his dialect
He was a different kind of man.

He traveled through this country
Walked many miles on this land
But, now he's in a place
Not built by the hands of man.

Gone away in body, still
Here in spirit and soul
He lived a comfortable life
Days went by, as he grew old.

He worked from sun to sun
Made sure his job was done
Loved all of his children's
Children, as well as his stepson

With a heart pure as gold
His love he never told but,
Deep within our hearts we
Knew, no one was ever so true!

In remembrance of my father
4/ 14/ 21 – 1/ 8/ 96

With Love,

Oh Lover Of My Soul Part II

There once was a time when I had no one to hold and then came you into my life and touched my soul. The times that we shared were in my greatest despair I could depend on you to always be there. I held you tight, you lit up my life, your presence soothed my heart in the darkest hours of the night.

The more you came, the longer I wanted you to stay, my love for you grew stronger everyday. Your presence in my life changed my whole pathway . Oh lover of my soul of your love I did behold. The love you gave could not be replaced. You engulfed my soul in your time and space.

After so long, something went wrong. You rocked my world and my life was in a whirl, round and around I went. You slowly destroyed everything in my world. I looked around, no one or nothing was there. You took everything from me you no longer cared. Oh lover of my soul you left me bare.

Now the time has come for me to let you go. I've grown sick and tried and developed cirrhosis of the soul. The hour has come for me to say goodbye. To be with you, I will die. I've turned my will over to a power greater than you. And just for today I choose to live, learn and love God's way.

POWERS AND PRINCIPALITIES

Powers and Principalities
The powers that be
Operates in the Spirit realm
Of this universe
That resides over you and me

Powers and Principalities
The powers that be
Are aware of everything
That is taking place
Nowhere can you be free.

Nowhere can you flee from
Its powers, nor hide from
The principalities so
Where can you go, from
It's Spirit if it surrounds
The universal cosmology

Prayer

March 14, 2007 (One day before Pre-lim hearing)

A Prayer Request for Antwan

The Lord will work out her plans for my life. For your faithful Love, O Lord endures forever. Look down upon my sorrows and rescue Antwan O Lord. Argue Antwans' case and take his side. Protect his life as you promised Lord, how great is your Mercy! In your justice give Antwan back his life. Give back his life because of your unfailing love. Stand ready to help Antwan for he has chosen to follow all of your commandments.

But the Lord is good. He has cut the chains used by the ungodly to bind Antwan. O God, whom I praise. Don't stand silent and aloof while the wicked slander Antwan and tell lies about him. Amen

Psalms138: 8   Psalms 154

Psalms 119   Psalms 129   Psalms 109

51

Ancestors Come Now!

Madonna and Jesus, come now! Maat and Tehuti, come now! Green Tara, come now!

Thank you, Mother and Father God.

Expect a miracle and hope for the best. Speak Lord, for the witness. Speak Lord for the prosecutor. Speak Lord for the Judge. Speak Lord for the Lawyer. Protect Antwan's life as you promised. Do not let anyone lie against Antwan.

Bless the Lord O' my Soul and Bless the Lord O' Antwans' Soul and all that is within us. Thank you Lord for all of your goodness and grace. O' Lord, please argue Antwans' case and take his side. Do not let any false witness bear lies against Antwan. Praises are due to the Most High God whose mercy and strength endures forever!

Ancestors, Ancestors, come now, come quickly! Do not let any bear false witness against Antwan. Ancestors, come quickly, we need your help and assistance.
Ahshay.

The Lord is blessing us right now. She is our strength and our strong hold. In whom can we put our trust in, but the Lord Almighty! She is the one who has planned and purposed our lives. Lord Shine your light on Antwan and plead his case. Let the tongue of the liar stutter and turn their lies into truth.

O' Lord, please, plead his case and help the Lawyers plead his case with your truth, wisdom, understanding and knowledge. Let the truth come to the light as promised. Let the prosecutor see that Antwan is not present with any weapons formed against him. Make it known that the witnesses tells lies and are confused in thoughts.

O' Lord, Mother God, teach the prosecutor the appropriate ways to assist in Antwans' defense, for Antwan has chosen to obey the Lord's commandments.

The officers are confounded by the evidence and reports of the case. The Lord is pleading Antwans' case and the words of the officer are on the good side of Antwan. God has shown favor towards Antwan and will be compassionate towards his case.

The witnesses are telling lies and the court cannot hold Antwan accountable for the charges. The detective is speaking slander about Antwan and cannot testify against him because he knows Antwan has an innocent soul.

Plans go wrong for the lack of advice. Many counselors bring success. Everyone enjoys a fitting reply; it is wonderful to say the right thing at the right time. Everything has already been decided. It was known long ago, what each person would be. So there is no sense of arguing with God about your destiny.

Sorrow is better than laughter, for sadness has a refining influence on us.

Finishing is better than starting. Patience is better than pride.

Notice the way God does things, then fall into line. Don't fight the ways of God, for who can straighten out what He has made crooked?

O' Lord, hear Antwans' plea for righteousness and justice. Listen to his cry for help. Declare Antwan innocence, for you know those who do right. Amen

Proverbs 15, Eccl. 6, Psalms 17
March 16, 2007

But the Lord is good. He has cut the chains used by the ungodly to bind Antwan. The plans devised by the prosecutor against Antwan go wrong for lack of advice. Many counselors bring success. Everyone enjoys a fitting reply; it is wonderful to say the right thing at the right time. The court has already been denied. God has promised to protect Antwans' life. How great is your Mercy! In your justice, give Antwan back his life. O God whom I praise, don't stand silent and aloof while the wicked slander Antwan and tell lies about him. Amen

Faith is the substance of things hoped for and the evidence of things not seen. The officers remain confounded by the evidence and their reports. God is pleading Antwans' case. The officials are on the good side of Antwan. Amen
As it is written, so it is!

April 2, 2007

God has shown favor towards Antwan and he will be compassionate towards this case. The DA and the People have the word of the Lord on their lips and cannot lie. The court officials and the judge stand on the law of the Lord. The laws of man go wrong. Let the tongue of the liars stutter and turn their lies into truth. Come now, O Ancestors and the God of my Father's Father, The God of my Mother's Mother, come to his rescue and to his assistance. Mother of God, Mother of Mary and Mother of Jesus, Please tie the tongues of all the liars. It's God whom I praise.

Recognition of Father/Mother God

A s I look around and within, I can't help but recognize how great thou art. Oh Lord, my Creator and Maker, Father and Mother God working together forming all of us as one. Oh Lord, how great and mighty you truly are; simply wonderful, thou art totally magnificent. I glory at all the work you have done. I'm grateful, forever mindful and so appreciative. I am grateful for all that you have done for me. Oh Lord, I am grateful for your every deed, providing for me everything I need and more. As my heavenly Father God and nurturing Mother God, you have designed and cultivated this beautiful world all around and within. By the power of your divine word, you created and made the fullness of the world and the host within.

Mother/Father God, you are so marvelous, clothed with Mercy and Grace. I cannot help but continuously praise you all the days of my life. As I take a look within, I am always knowing that I'm never without the manifestation of you Heavenly Father and you Holy Mother. You fashioned and formed me with your creative hands, to walk with you on my right hand, giving me strength to eternally depend on you always.

I am grateful and forever mindful of your power within my soul. I cannot imagine the depth of your Love that you have created beneath the sea or the heights of your Love above the stars. How great you are. Creator and Maker, My Father and My Mother created as one. Made in the likeness and image of my Mother just as you are. I am woman made in the image and likeness of my Father, just as you are. So too am I. I am one, you are one, my Father, my Mother, how great you are.

Praises are divinely and continuously owed to you for all that you are and for all that you have done, from as far as the East is to the West, from Sun to Sun you are worthy to be praised by everyone. Thank you for your guiding light and love sent from above, below and within.

SHADOWS

WHEN WE WERE ONLY SHADOWS
MERE THOUGHTS IN EACH OTHER MINDS.
WE LONGED DEEPLY TO BE TOGETHER
ONCE AGAIN IN THIS LIFE TIME

WE SEARCHED FOR EACH OTHER DAILY
L00KING HERE AND THERE WE GLIMPSED
AT EACH OTHERS INNER SOUL
EVEN THOUGH WE WERE NOT THERE

WHEN WE WERE ONLY SHADOWS,
PERFECT LOVERS FOR ONE ANOTHER
WE EMBRACED THE SHADOWS OF OUR
MINDS WITHOUT REMEMBRANCE
OF ANY SPACE OR TIME

IN LOVING MEMORY

SPIRIT

SPIRIT ONLY SPEAKS TO SPIRIT
WITH HUMAN EARS WE HEAR
THE DIALOGUE WITH THE SPIRIT
FROM THE SPIRIT WILL REST MY SOUL

SPIRIT SPEAKS TO SPIRIT
TELLS ME WHICH WAY TO GO
WHERE EVER MY SPIRIT LEADS ME
MY SOUL AND I SHALL GO

TO WALK AND TALK WITH
THE SPIRIT – TRUTH WILL BE REVEALED
TO HONOR GOD IN TRUTH AND SPIRIT
IS THE IDEAL WAY TO LIVE

IN TRUTH AND SPIRIT

MERCEDES A. BROWN

SUNSHINE

The Sun as it rises
To it's highest peak
Everyday-whether the
Sun shines or not
At high noon the
Sun is at its best

In the midst of
My life, the Sun
Replicates my position
As it sets in the West
While I am on
My bending knees

As I go down
In prayer to praise
The beautiful wonders
Of all the land,
I glorify your blessedness!

SURFACE LANDMARKS REARRANGED

Life takes us through many changes
And often rearranges the familiar
Places in our minds and hearts but
Never forgetting that old landmark.

The surface landmark is the object of
Our affection that represents the love in
Space and time that we shared in solid
Form from the very start

In memory of a place where we used to be
Surface landmarks rearranged the
Outward appearance of the home we
Loved and shared by the sea.

Surface landmarks rearranged
Changing the way things used to be
Tearing down and building up
Creating something new to see.

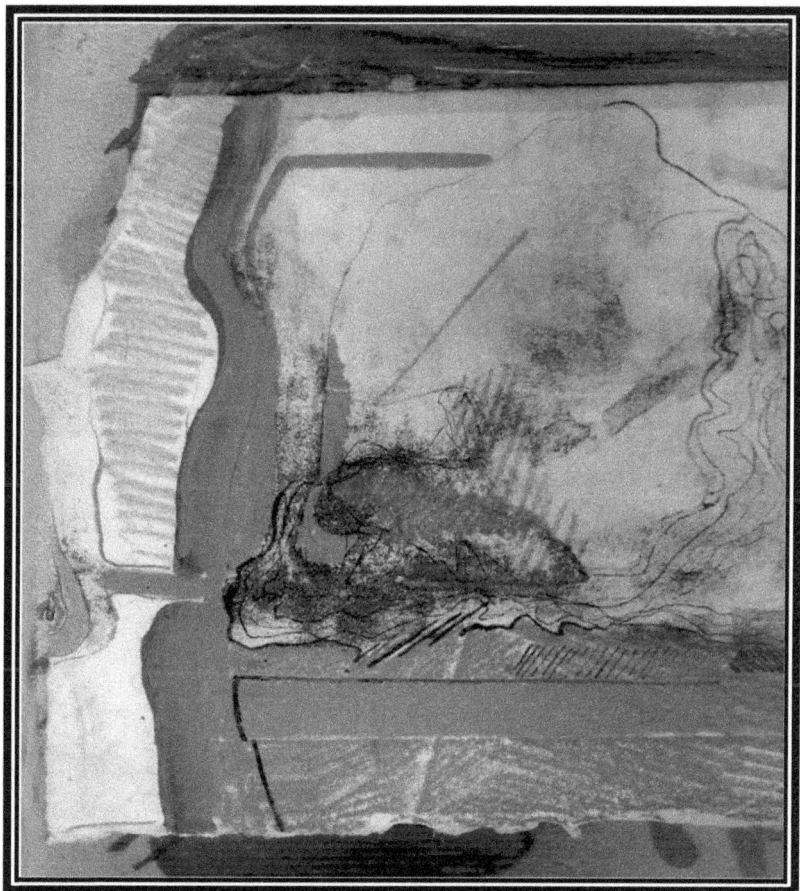

(Sweet Holy Spirit Mother Goddess)

Oh sweet Holy Spirit, Mother Goddess, you are the mother of all. Out of your soul you brought forth every living thing in divine order and perfection. You gave nourishment and birth to all of our Father God creations- bestowing life, health, prosperity, in right thinking and truth. With your loving tender mercies you have cleansed our spirit and body with your precious living waters. You wash our Divine Mind, Soul and Body, as a Mother would cleanse her newborn baby. You gently wash away our iniquities and transgressions, restoring our bodies in perfect health and well-being. Energizing us with your strength and power you allow each of us to become new in our bodies and soul. Blessing us with new hopes and desires. Filling us with your confidence and esteem. Our cup is running over with your love.

Thank you for the knowledge, wisdom, and understanding of your blessed presence. Thank you for allowing us to remember to praise you and worship you for being so forgiving of our wrong doings.

I will glorify you Mother/Father God. I will magnify you. I will speak of your comforting, and sustaining love that gives Life, Health, Wealth, Love more abundantly.

As Above So Below and Within, - Forever Amen.

My Blessed Holy Mother God

I praise you, glorify you, and lift you above all men and women. You are the Mother of all the lands and no one can deny you of your power in this world to heal and nurture recognizing the love that exists in all mothers. You exemplify your presence and wisdom. I'm troubled by the reaction of your child who chooses not to believe in your existence as we do in our earthly mother.

Sweet Holy Spirit Mother God One

Thank you for your strength in my weakness. You have created me and know all of me more than I know myself. You are acquainted in all of my ways. Thank you for your divine wisdom on every level of my existence. Thank you for giving me the mind to solve the many problems that I am faced with. Thank you for your understanding and knowledge. For there is no one who can help me, cares for me, or can hear my cry as you can. I am your child, a direct offspring of your nature, in its divinity. I do have complete trust, and faith in your doings, I rejoice in you. Thank you for your divine intervention in the affairs and transaction of those things that are being threatened by their very existence in my life. Only you can work it out for my good. Help me to remove all that is unpleasing to you. Only you can teach me the divine and correct way to do your will. Praises are bestowed upon you forever, and ever.

Sweet Holy Spirit Mother God

I come before you in praise and thanksgiving to say thank you- thank you for blessing us with your son who laid down his life for our upmost and highest good. I bless you for the sacrifices you have made on behalf, of all of creation you continue to remain silent as we go about our daily duties without any thought of your blessedness on the throne of god. I bless him for your presence and the awareness of your existence in my life throughout the heavens and the earth – thank you!

Sweet Holy Spirit Mother God – I glorify at the manisfestation of your presence in my life. I marvel at the wonders of your Holy Spirit. I bless the moment you came to my awareness. You came to me in my hour of need to let me know that you were there to assist me when I was sick and afflicted. You delivered me and nourished me back to life. When I was abused, you repaired my soul. I glorify and adore you, I praise you and thank you for your blessedness and your holiness. For the rest of my life, I will continue to acknowledge you as my Sweet Holy Spirit Mother God, the oneness of all creation.

And so it is!

Sweet Holy Spirit

Sweet Holy Spirit, Mother of all Mothers, Mother of our Father's Fathers. You are the Mother of all good things known to all of mankind. I am forever grateful for your loving kindness in my life. Thank you, for your presence in my awareness for that which constantly reminds me of your great power and wisdom. After all that I have seen and heard in the past, I'm in honor and reverence of your being as the female energy in all manifestations.

Thanksgiving

Oh give thanks unto the Lord

Every day of your life

Be not like the sinful ones

Giving thanks every once and awhile

Give thanks whether you're up or down.

Give thanks all-year-round giving

Thanks in everything

Not only for one day

Shout and make a joyful sound

For Mother God is worthy to be

Praised.

Everyday, not just holidays.

Every morning, noon and night

Even when the sun goes down

Lift up your voice and shout,

Thank you!

There is a River Flowing

Far away from this troubled place, there is a river flowing. Across this land that we know of there is a river flowing. Flowing in a distant place, a peaceful river is flowing. A place that my spirit and soul knows where it exists; calming my body, comforting my soul, in a peaceful place, a quiet place where a river flows. The river flows in Paradise.

Know That You Are

Know that you are

That which is love

Created to Love-

Created to be loved,

By your "self" and

Everyone else.

So do that great thing

In which only you can do,

Make that contribution

To all of Man, including yourself!

And know that you are.

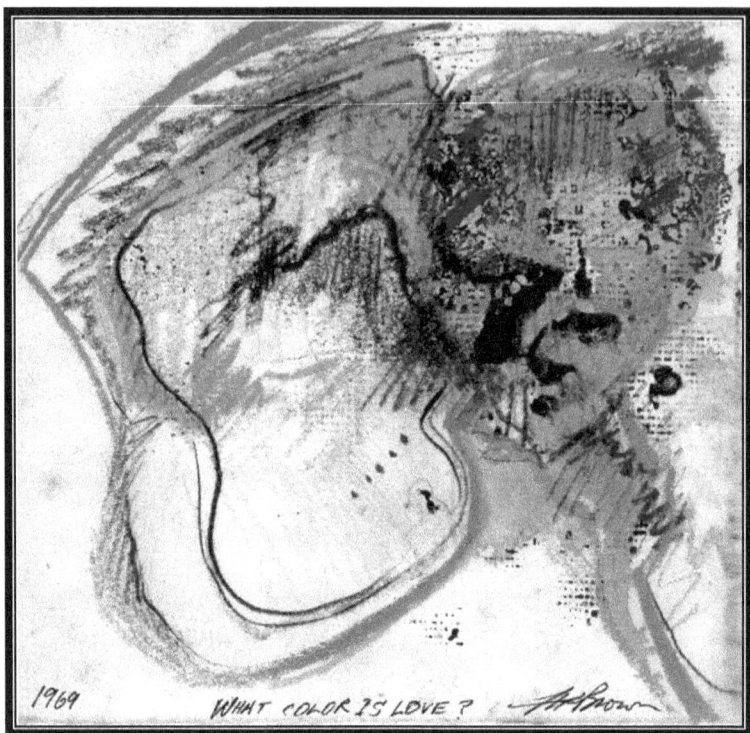

1969   WHAT COLOR IS LOVE ?

What Color Is Love?

Black is evil
White is good
Pure and clean
Red is bloods
Blue is crips
Yellow is golden
Green is Energy
What color is Love?

Purple is royal
Orange is the sunset
Green can mean life
Black is death
Tell me
What color is Love?

White is light
Blue is peace
Yellow is jealous
Green is envy
Red is passion
Pretty is pink
What color is Love?
Besides you and me?
That's the color of Love.

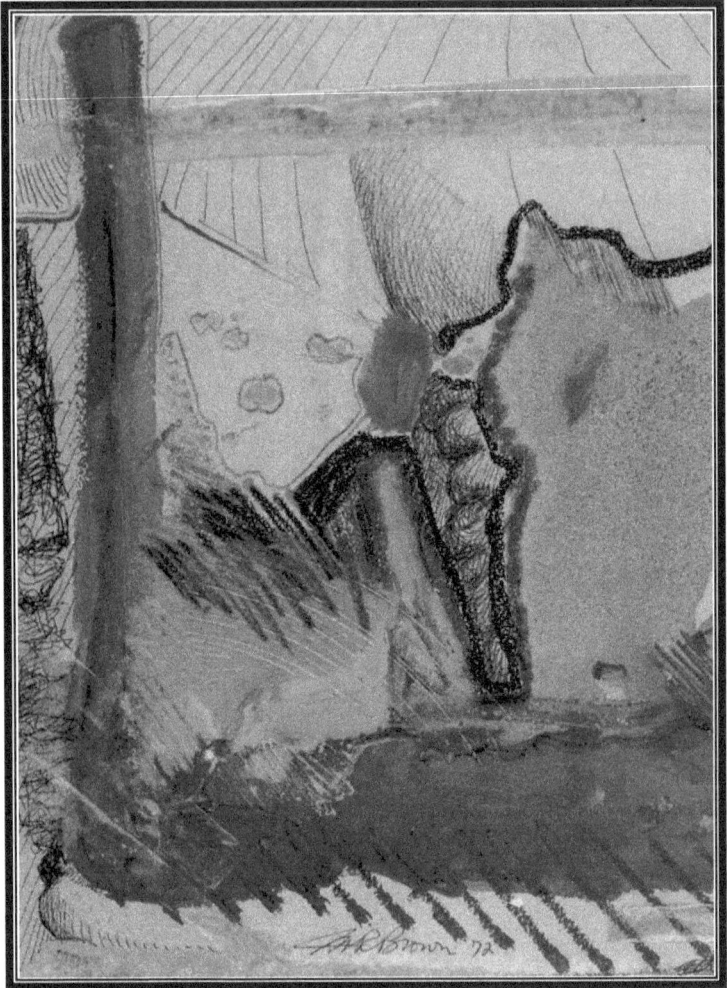

I Do Shine

I am a direct descendant of the universe:
All that's within and about it, I am.
Yes, I am the sun, moon and the stars.

As the sun, I rise and I set, like the moon,
I come and I go and,
As the shadows of the stars at high
Noon, yes, I am too. I do shine!

In the radiance of the sunlight which
Enlightens me, there appears the sunset
In the distant horizon to bring my darkness
And so it is, I do shine!

Just as in my darkness,
The lunar cycle comes around and it goes,
And then the moonlight comes about and enlightens me,
As above, so below I, too, shine!

The dawning of a new day
And in the brightness of golden sun-rays
Be that as it may, as the stars shine always-I do shine!

So, in the dept of my darkness,
As in the absence of the moonlight
Like the stars hidden-I do shine!

JOURNEYING

Being a resident in a community filled with crime, violence and uncertainty, it's rather difficult to walk outside my door without a destination. It is important for me to always know where I am going. There is a saying, "If you don't know where you have been, how can you know where you are going?" To complete this assignment proved to be in and of itself somewhat stressful. For me to go for a walk without an outer goal or destination was difficult. There are a few things to consider safety, time and place.

In my immediate neighborhood, there are a lot of dogs and I have to be careful as to not cross their paths. You have to watch where you are going while you are on your journey. There are also a lot of suspicious people who are homeless and linger hopelessly around on the streets, in the park, on corners, standing in front of you, walking behind you, some here and there. Who can you trust? As I go on my journey and walk in the community, I walk without fear. I know that my God walks with me. I can walk in the "hood" in peace because I am there for a reason a purpose.

As I walk on my journey, I walk in spirit and in truth. I leave my home saying to myself, may God bless me in my coming in and in my going out. I utter to myself, may He keep me from all hurt, harm and danger. May His ten thousand angels encamp themselves about me. As I walk in the spirit, I am in constant praise and worship to the utmost and the highest power that be, giving reverence and thanksgivings. On my journey, as I walk in truth, I see that which is true, I hear that which is true and I speak that which my spirit has opened my ears to hear, the wisdom that is spoken to me and confirmed as true.

On my journey, as I walk in spirit and in truth, I am made aware of the scripture that speaks of the Earth and the fullness thereof, all belongs to God. As I walk and observe nature in silence, I am reminded of the creative power of God that resides within me. As I continue to walk and observe the debris on the streets and in the parks, I am also prompted to observe the debris in me; and the need to cleanse myself, and heal myself, along with my community. As I continue walking, I think of ways I can cleanse myself by changing my diet and by changing the way I view the world.

Oh Lover Of My Soul

Oh Lover of my soul
There is a part in he who
Wishes to be free
Please tell me of that
Part in he who
Why or why wishes
To, be free?

That part in he who
Wishes to be free
Merely wastes time
By and by wanting
What is naught!

To be free is an
Expression that can
Only be sought,
Because nothing on
Earth is free to be
Anything other than
A manifestation of me

I am she in he
Who wishes to be free!
Spirit and Soul combined
In the body as three
And it is not until
His duty unto me is
Complete, until then
He cannot be free!

So know with one mind
The nature of mankind
To create and to love
All of God's beauty
Not only that which is
Above and below, but within
Created simply to love
And be loved.

THE WHISPERS OF MAAT

Listen to the Whispers of Maat
As she blows the sounds of Truth
Whispering, blowing, humming
Of ancient truths in the winds

Open your eyes to Maat
Change your mind and see
A Maatian revelation only
A few of you will find
In yours Intimate relations with Maat
She will blow your mind.

Hear the rightness of the
Righteous ways we are
To travel on this road,
Maat will guide and direct you
On the right path we are to go.

Just listen to the sounds of Maat
As she speaks silent truths
It's our time to abide to the Laws
Of Maat that stand for Justice
All of the time for me and you

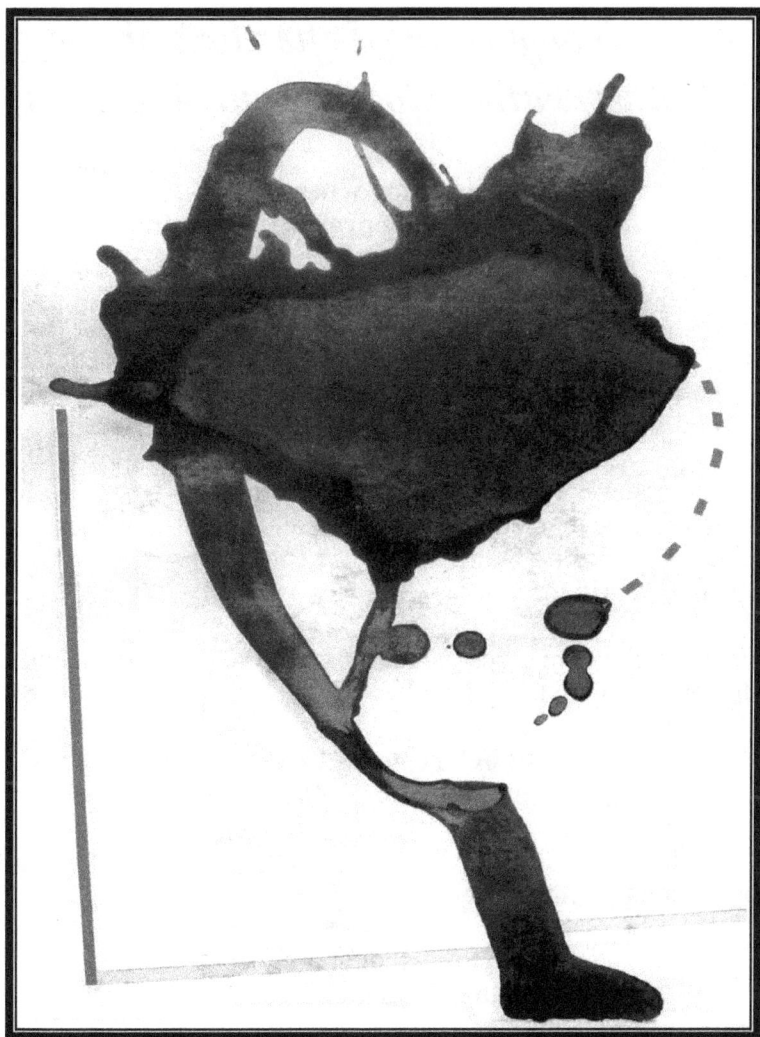

Thoughts and Reflections of Mother/Father God and our Ancestors

**Every morning when I wake,
I keep the following prayer in my mind:**

I have a divine essence, an individualized part of God within myself, and I serve as Mother/Father God's instrument. Each person, with whom I come into contact today, also has a divine essence. I will treat each person kindly with this thought in mind.

Whenever I suffer from doubts, worries or other negative thoughts, I recognize and accept them humbly as messages from my ancestors. I surrender these concerns to Mother/Father God to be purified.

I will do my best today to serve as an instrument of Mother/Father God, along with my ancestors, who are within me.

**Every night before going to bed, I offer this
prayer of gratitude to Mother/Father God:**

Thank you for allowing me to serve in your divine work today along with the knowledge of my ancestors.

**Acknowledgement of
Mother/Father God and Our Ancestors:**

I humbly acknowledge Mother God as the Mother of Jesus and all mankind. I acknowledge Mother/Father God as my Creator and Savior.

I also acknowledge that the feelings, thoughts and sufferings whether from illness, financial difficulty and conflict, are manifesting in me; Here at this moment, are reflections of my ancestors' suffering that are seeking salvation.

80

Dear ancestors who are now manifesting in me, together, let us surrender our suffering to Mother/Father God, our Creator and Savior to be purified, forgiven and saved.

Our Creator and Savior, please purify, forgive and save the feelings, thoughts and sufferings that are messages from my ancestors who are now at this moment manifesting in me.

Mother/Father God, our Creator and Savior, please manifest your Will right here, right now and forever.

Revised Sonen Prayer

PRAYERS TO MOTHER GOD

SWEET HOLY SPIRIT, MOTHER GOD.

PLEASE – HAVE MERCY UPON ME
AND FORGIVE ME FOR ALL THE DAYS OF MY LIFE
THAT I HAVE IGNORED YOU AND
ACT AS IF I DID NOT
KNOW YOU – WHEN IT IS YOU WHO GIVES US LIFE
AND NOURISHES OUR BODIES WITH THE FOOD
THAT COMES FROM YOUR EARTH.
IT IS YOU WHO CLOTHE ME
WITH THE MATERIALS
THAT COMES FROM YOUR BODY,
YOUR LAND AND EARTH.
OH HOW I LOVE YOU AND ADORE YOU
SWEET HOLY SPIRIT, MOTHER GOD.

SWEET HOLY SPIRIT MOTHER GOD.
THANK YOU FOR YOUR PRESENCE IN MY LIFE
THANK YOU FOR YOUR HOLINESS, IN ALL ITS
BEAUTY AND ITS MAJESTY
I TURN TO YOU IN THIS HOUR OF NEED AND
ASK THAT YOU TO ASSIST ME IN THE WORK THAT
I MUST DO. I NEED YOUR SWEET HOLY SPIRIT AND

THE GRACE THAT FATHER GOD HAS BESTOWED
UPON YOU; IN YOUR LOVELINESS AND IN YOUR
GENTLENESS YOU
SECRETLY NOURISH THE WORLD WITHOUT ANY
ACKNOWLEDGMENT OR
RECOGNITION FROM YOUR CHILDREN.
BECAUSE OF YOUR WISDOM AND GRACE,
I HONOR YOU, BLESS YOU AND THANK YOU.
SWEET HOLY SPIRIT, MOTHER GOD
THANK YOU FOR BLESSING ME WITH THE
KNOWLEDGE, WISDOM AND UNDERSTANDING OF,
YOUR BLESSEDNESS AND YOUR PRESENCE IN MY
LIFE. THANK YOU FOR GIVING ME THE SPIRIT TO
REMEMBER TO PRAISE YOU AND WORSHIP YOU FOR
BEING SO FORGIVING OF OUR FORGETFULNESS.

I WILL GLORIFY AND MAGNIFY YOU IN YOUR
LOVING KINDNESS. I WILL SPEAK OF YOUR
COMFORTING AND SUSTAINING LOVE AS YOU
CONTINUE TO GIVE LIFE, HEALTH, WEALTH, AND
LOVE MORE ABUNDANTLY, I WILL REMEMBER
YOUR PRESENCE IN MY LIFE.

My Beloved Sweet Holy Spirit Mother God

I PRAISE YOU, GLORIFY YOU AND LIFT YOU ABOVE ALL MEN AND WOMEN. YOU ARE THE MOTHER OF ALL THE LAND AND NO ONE CAN DENY YOUR POWERS IN THIS WORLD, TO HEAL THE BROKEN HEARTED AND NURTURE THE WEAK. THE LOVE THAT IMMINATES FROM YOU; EXEMPLIFY YOUR PRESENCE AND WISDOM.

I AM TROUBLED BY THE ACTIONS OF YOUR GRAND CHILDREN WHO CHOSE NOT TO RECOGNIZE AND BELIEVE IN YOUR EXISTENCE AS A REPRESENTATIVE OF MOTHER EARTH. I ASK THAT YOU OPEN THEIR EYES THAT THEY MAY SEE THE GLORY OF YOUR DIVINE. EXPAND THEIR MINDS THAT THEY MAY ENGULF THE KNOWLEDGE AND UNDERSTANDING OF YOUR BEING. INCREASE THEIR AWARENESS OF YOUR BEAUTY AND PRESENCE IN THEIR IMMEDIATE ENVIRONMENT AND THE ENTIRE UNIVERSE.

I WILL PRAISE YOU, GLORIFY YOU, AND LIFT YOU ABOVE ALL MEN!

"If You Were Me"

How could it be – the whole
world is looking at me?
How would it be if you were me?
How should it be- when I, a warrior, a chief,
A mighty man of valor!
Am pursuing the last miles
Of freedom of my life!

With a glimpse of today being radiant by the sun
Yet, it's so dark.
Thoughts of yesterday, being
Showered with beauty, power, wealth, strength,
Romance and with so much love and memories
Of death, only dread for tomorrow, for there
Is no hope for me!

But now! Faith is the substance of things hoped
For and the evidence of things not seen!

LIFE IS ART

Life is a picture
Just waiting for
You to paint it
Color it, as you will
Taint it if you may.
No matter how you
Paint it; it's just
The way art is
Sunshine, Purple Skies
And rainbows in the night,
Regardless how it looks
Depends on your creative
Insight.

Prayer for My Sons

Mother Father God, it is you who has allowed

Me to dwell in your house of Forgiveness and

Faithfulness. Please hear my prayer as I seek

Your guidance and protection for my Sons

Who are suffering for many reasons and for many

causes?

They are in need of your effectiveness

in the purpose of

Their lives have mercy upon them. Bless them

Mind, heart and soul, to know that you are

All they will ever need to progress through this

Promise land. Help them to know your ways.

Amen

Dedicated to Deon Laquise and Antwan Bernard.